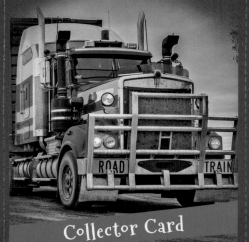

MIGHTY TRUCKS

Collector Card

MIGHTY TRUCKS

Collector Card

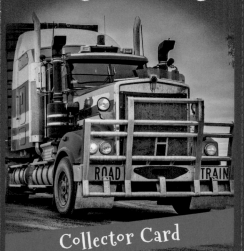

MIGHTY TRUCKS

Collector Card

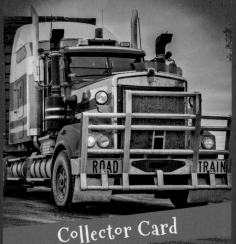

MIGHTY TRUCKS

Collector Card

LeTourneau L-2350

This vehicle holds the world record for the biggest earth mover.

	SCORE
ENGINE POWER: 1715 kW	6
MAX. LOAD WEIGHT: 72,500 kg	6
LENGTH: 20.3 m	9
TOP SPEED: 16.9 km/h	1

Liebherr T284

An awesome mining truck that carries really heavy loads.

	SCORE
ENGINE POWER: 3000 kW	8
MAX. LOAD WEIGHT: 363,000 kg	9
LENGTH: 14.5 m	5
TOP SPEED: 54 km/h	3

This vehicle can drive over, through and up, and survive almost anything.

ENGINE POWER: 239 kW	2
MAX. LOAD WEIGHT: 10 soldiers	2
LENGTH: 6.7 m	3
TOP SPEED: 105 km/h	8

Toyota Hilux

A version of this truck was the first vehicle to be driven to the North Pole.

	SCORE
ENGINE POWER: 207 kW	1
MAX. LOAD WEIGHT: 1390 kg	4
LENGTH: 5.26 m	1
TOP SPEED: 175 km/h	10

It's all about...

MIGHTY
TRUCKS

ROAD   TRAIN

KINGFISHER

First published 2016 by Kingfisher
an imprint of Macmillan Children's Books
20 New Wharf Road, London N1 9RR
Associated companies throughout the world
www.panmacmillan.com

Series editor: Sarah Snashall
Series design: Anthony Hannant (LittleRedAnt)
Adapted from an original text by Brenda Stones

ISBN 978-0-7534-3938-8

Copyright © Macmillan Publishers International Ltd 2016

9 8 7 6 5 4 3 2 1

1TR/1115/WKT/UG/128MA

A CIP catalogue record for this book is available from the British Library.

Printed in China

Picture credits
The Publisher would like to thank the following for permission to reproduce their material.
Top = t; Bottom = b; Centre = c; Left = l; Right = r
Cover, p1 Shutterstock/Marco Saracco; Back cover Shutterstock/Alaettin YILDIRIM;
Pages 2–3, 26–27, 30–31 Shutterstock/Natursports; 4–5 Shutterstock/Fernando Rodrogues;
5t Shutterstock/Chalyapruk Chanwatthana; 5b LeTourneau; 6 Shutterstock/hydyl;
7t Dreamstime/Lcjtripod; 7b Shutterstock/Neale Cousland; 8 Shutterstock/Vytautas Kielaitis;
9t Shutterstock/TFoxFoto; 9b Alamy/Tim Scrivener; 10 Alamy/imageBROKER; 11t Getty/Gilles
Bassignac; 11 Alamy/Porky Pies Photography; 12–13 Alamy/Gary K Smith; 13t Shutterstock/
StevanZZ; 13b Tate & Lyle Ltd; 14 Shutterstock/abutyrin; 15t Shutterstock/Kustov;
15b Liebherr; 16 Alamy/Alvey & Towers Picture Library; 17 Shutterstock/zorandim; 18 Getty/
Eric Piermont/AFP; 19t Alamy/Kevin Wheal; 20 Shutterstock/Mike Brake; 21 Rosenbauer
International AG; 22 Shutterstock/Vladimir Nenezic; 23t Shutterstock/Benoit Daoust;
23b Alamy/Tengku Mohd Yusof; 24 Alamy/AF Archive; 25t Shutterstock/Pieter Beens;
25b Alamy/Michele Burgess; 27 Alamy/Peter de Clercq; 28 Shutterstock/Taina Sohlman;
29t Alamy/dbimages; 29b Getty/Asahi Shimbun; 32 Shutterstock/Rodrigo Garrido.
Cards: Front tr Liebherr; br Shutterstock/Rodrigo Garrido; Back tl Alamy/pbpgalleries;
tr Komatsu; bl Liebherr; br Belaz Trucks Americas.

Front cover: A huge truck pulls the trailers of an Australian road train.

CONTENTS

Trucks everywhere

A truck is a strong vehicle that carries things. Lorries carry goods from place to place, dumper trucks carry rocks, fire engines carry water and tow trucks pull planes and cars. There are small trucks, such as golf buggies, and huge trucks, such as mining loaders.

A forklift truck moves a container at a port.

SPOTLIGHT: LeTourneau L-2350

Famous for:	world's largest loader
Strength:	2300 horsepower
Bucket capacity:	72,500 kg
Use:	mining

The LeTourneau L-2350 is the biggest earth mover in the world.

All kinds of goods

Most of the trucks you see on the road are lorries. They carry goods from one place to another. Sometimes they carry food; sometimes they collect containers from ships; sometimes they are used to help people move to a new home.

A lorry waits at a sea port for a container to be loaded onto it.

Lorries can carry enormous loads.

FACT...

Australian road trains usually pull up to six
trailers. In 2006, the longest-ever road train
pulled 112 trailers – but only for 100 metres.

Tricky loads

Some things are tricky to move, so special lorries are designed just for the job. Timber trucks have a flat base, open sides and wheels that can drive in forests. Car transporters have ramps, and animal transporters have non-slip floors.

Timber trucks transport logs from the forest to paper mills and furniture factories.

Sheep transporters have gaps in the side to let in fresh air.

FACT...

Cars drive up ramps onto a car transporter. The first row of cars is then hauled up to allow another row to drive on below.

Life on the road

Some long-distance lorry drivers spend most of their life on the road. At night, the driver parks the lorry and sleeps in the cab.

FACT...

Many lorry drivers drive for thousands of kilometres, sometimes over dangerous and remote roads. In winter, some roads cross frozen lakes.

Long-distance lorry drivers have a bed, a mini-kitchen and a television in their cab.

This road in Bolivia is known as 'Death Road'. It is rarely more than three metres wide and has no guard rails.

Liquids on the move

Liquids such as oil, water or milk are moved in special trucks called tankers. Milk is taken from farms to dairies in insulated tankers that can hold up to 30,000 litres of milk. When a ship carrying oil docks in a port, pipes are connected to the ship to fill the road tankers waiting alongside.

Milk tankers collect milk from dairy farms every day.

Petrol tankers collect petrol and diesel from refineries to deliver to petrol stations.

BONALLACK & SONS 268

MANUFACTURED AS USUAL

LYLE'S GOLDEN SYRUP

BETTER THAN BUTTER

This early truck was used to transport Lyle's Golden Syrup.

The biggest!

The biggest trucks are used to transport loads around mines and quarries. Huge cranes break up rocks in a quarry and then enormous dumper trucks carry them away. Mines use enormous wheel loaders and dumper trucks to move the coal.

A quarry crane can move slabs of rock as big as a car.

Dumper trucks as big as a house are used at coal mines.

SPOTLIGHT: Liebherr T284

Famous for:	world's second largest mining truck
Strength:	up to 4000 horsepower
Capacity:	363,000 kg of coal
Use:	mines and quarries

FACT...

Mining trucks are too heavy to travel on the road and are transported around by lorries.

On the building site

Lots of different trucks drive around a building site. Diggers dig up the ground using metal buckets, and bulldozers push the earth around. There are also concrete mixers, crane lorries, dumper trucks and excavators.

The concrete comes to the building site in a concrete mixer.

FACT...

Instead of wheels, a bulldozer has caterpillar treads to stop it slipping in the mud.

A truck with a crane attachment lifts building materials.

Tough trucks

Moving soldiers and equipment in the most dangerous places in the world needs tough trucks. They must be extra-strong to protect the soldiers inside, and have tough wheels and suspension to cope with rough ground.

Armies have small patrol trucks, larger troop carriers and special armoured mine clearers.

Mine clearers move over rocky land to clear any bombs.

A patrol buggy can drive quickly over rough ground.

SPOTLIGHT: Renault VAB III

Famous for:	able to drive on land and in water
Strength:	320 horsepower
Capacity:	10 soldiers and kit
Top speed:	105 km/h

19

Fire engines

Fire engines carry firefighters, hoses, ladders, axes and other firefighting items to help put out a fire. Inside the truck is a huge tank of water; around the sides are many long hoses.

Extra-long ladders allow firefighters to reach tall buildings.

SPOTLIGHT: The Stinger

Famous for:	piercing tool that cuts metal
Strength:	1260 horsepower
Capacity:	max. reach of 13.8 metres
Use:	aircraft fires

FACT...

The Stinger is used at airports around the world, including Berlin in Germany. It has a spike to pierce the body of an aeroplane and inject fire-stopping chemicals inside.

Road works

When a new road is made, first a bulldozer prepares the ground and makes the shape of the road. Next, a dumper truck brings gravel and places it on the road.

Lastly, a truck pours concrete or tarmac on the road and a road roller helps to create a smooth surface.

A heavy road roller flattens the bed of a new road.

During bad weather, snowploughs work to clear the roads.

Road sweepers sweep and suck up leaves and rubbish from the road.

Tow trucks

Trucks are very strong and can be used to pull things along. Small pickup trucks can tow caravans or trailers. Larger tow trucks can pull aeroplanes.

FACT...

The first tow truck was made in 1916 when Ernest Holmes attached three poles and a pulley to his 1913 Cadillac.

Tow Mater, from the film *Cars*, is probably the most famous tow truck in the world.

A low truck can slip underneath the nose of a plane and push it back from the parking gate.

SPOTLIGHT: Toyota Hilux

Famous for:	being almost indestructible!
Capacity:	two pallets (or 1 camel)
Strength:	169 horsepower
Use:	personal

Monster trucks

Special tracks with ramps are built for monster trucks to ride on.

FACT...

The original monster truck was created by Bob Chandler in 1974. It was called Bigfoot. One version of Bigfoot had 3-metre-high wheels.

What do you get when you add huge wheels, great suspension and bright colours to a pickup truck? A monster truck! A monster truck is a show truck designed for stunts and displays such as riding over obstacles and crushing other vehicles.

Monster trucks crush caravans and sometimes even aeroplanes!

Rainbow colours

Most trucks are painted plain colours but there are some highly decorated trucks that would really put a smile on your face. Some are painted to advertise their contents in clever ways; others are painted just for fun.

Painted Pakistani trucks are known as jingle trucks.

FACT...

Truck painting is a popular form of art in Pakistan and Japan. Truck owners spend thousands of pounds painting their trucks and adding lights, statues and mirrors.

Japanese painted *dekatora* trucks use neon lights and ultraviolet lights.

GLOSSARY

bulldozer A truck with a wide metal bucket that moves and carries rock and soil.

cab The place in a truck where the driver sits.

car transporter A lorry that carries cars, usually between five and nine.

caterpillar treads A metal band of bumpy plates that move around sets of wheels to stop them slipping.

cement mixer A truck with a large mixer attachment that is used to carry cement.

concrete A mixture of stones and cement used to make roads and buildings.

container A large strong metal box used to move goods by road, rail, sea or air.

dumper truck A truck with an open back that can tilt to pour out its contents.

excavator A truck with a digging attachment.

forklift truck A truck that picks up heavy loads with two prongs.

golf buggy A small electric truck that carries players around a golf course.

loader A truck with a bucket on an arm that moves rubble or earth.

mine clearer A truck that clears bombs from an area.

parking gate The place where an aeroplane parks to drop off and collect passengers.

patrol buggy A small truck for searching an area in a war zone.

quarry An area where rock is collected from the ground.

remote Far from anywhere else.

suspension The springs and other metal parts that support a vehicle on its wheels.

tarmac A black, sticky mixture used to make roads.

troop carrier A truck that moves soldiers.

INDEX

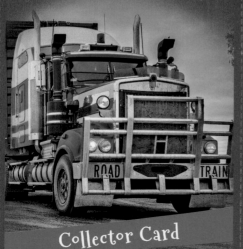

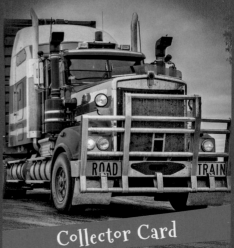

Bigfoot 17

This monster truck can jump over 14 cars placed side by side.

	SCORE
ENGINE POWER: 1304 kW	5
MAX. LOAD WEIGHT: 0	0
LENGTH: 5.49 m	2
TOP SPEED: 128 km/h	9

Komatsu 960E-1

One of the largest mining trucks in the world.

	SCORE
ENGINE POWER: 2610 kW	7
MAX. LOAD WEIGHT: 327,000 kg	8
LENGTH: 15.6 m	6
TOP SPEED: 64 km/h	4

Liebherr mobile crane LTM

The world's largest mobile crane has a 100-metre-long boom.

	SCORE
ENGINE POWER: 500 kW	3
MAX. LOAD WEIGHT: 1200 kg	3
LENGTH: 19.95 m	8
TOP SPEED: 80 km/h	5

Belaz 75710

The strongest truck in the world uses two engines to move.

	SCORE
ENGINE POWER: 4600 kW	10
MAX. LOAD WEIGHT: 450,000 kg	10
LENGTH: 20.6 m	10
TOP SPEED: 64 km/h	4

Collect all the titles in this series!

BEASTLY BUGS
FREE Collector Cards and Downloadable Audio!

DEADLY DINOSAURS
FREE Collector Cards and Downloadable Audio!

FANTASTIC FLIERS
FREE Collector Cards and Downloadable Audio!

FAST CARS
FREE Collector Cards and Downloadable Audio!

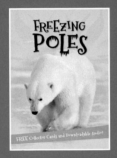

FREEZING POLES
FREE Collector Cards and Downloadable Audio!

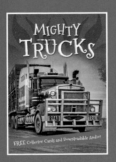

MIGHTY TRUCKS
FREE Collector Cards and Downloadable Audio!

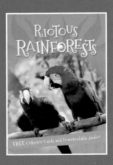

RIOTOUS RAINFORESTS
FREE Collector Cards and Downloadable Audio!

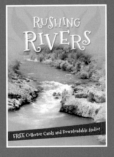

RUSHING RIVERS
FREE Collector Cards and Downloadable Audio!